This Walker book belongs to:

_____

_____

First published 1991 in *Greek Myths*
by Walker Books Ltd, 87 Vauxhall Walk, London SE11 5HJ

This edition published 2017

2 4 6 8 10 9 7 5 3 1

This book has been typeset in Goudy Old Style

Printed and bound in Great Britain by Clays Ltd, St Ives plc

British Library Cataloguing in Publication Data:
a catalogue record for this book is available from the British Library

ISBN 978-1-4063-7156-7

www.walker.co.uk

# Daedalus and Icarus
## & ##
## Orpheus and Eurydice

# Marcia Williams

WALKER BOOKS
AND SUBSIDIARIES
LONDON · BOSTON · SYDNEY · AUCKLAND

# Contents

## Daedalus and Icarus

# Orpheus and Eurydice

# Daedalus and Icarus

# Chapter One
# The King's Craftsman

Many years ago in Ancient Greece, a brilliant architect, inventor and craftsman, named Daedalus, worked for the King of Athens.

The temples he built were the most divine

ever seen, the chairs he made were the most
comfortable ever sat on, and his statues looked
so real that people believed they could talk.
Daedalus was famous throughout all of Greece
and was very proud of his work.

"I'm a genius," he would remark to his wife
… several times a day.

"Yes, dear, so you tell me," she would reply.

Daedalus had a young nephew, Talos, who was his apprentice. Talos was a very clever boy. Some said he was as clever as his uncle. Others said he was cleverer than his uncle, for he was already coming up with his own inventions.

"Look, Uncle!" said Talos after inventing

the potter's wheel. "You slap your clay down
on the wheel, spin it between your hands,
and hey presto – a pot!"

"I suppose it's not bad for a beginner,"
conceded Daedalus, grudgingly.

But when Talos invented the compass,
Daedalus flew into a fit of jealous rage.

"I think you need a compass Talos, for you
are getting a little above yourself," he warned.

Yet true genius cannot be contained and
Talos continued creating his wonders – so
much so, that the King of Athens began
to ask who this talented young designer was.

# Chapter Two
## Jealousy

Daedalus began to fear that Talos would replace him as the king's favourite. He became so jealous of Talos's genius that he pushed him

from the roof of a very high temple.

"Sorry, Talos, you are just too clever for your own good!" Daedalus said, as his poor nephew hurtled towards the ground.

Luckily, the goddess Athene, who sees all things, saw Talos spinning through the air and turned his spirit into a partridge which flew safely away. Meanwhile Talos's body

 14

crashed to the ground, where it lay, limp

and lifeless, for everyone to see. Daedalus,

fearing that the king would find out and pun-
ish him, fled with his son Icarus to the court
of King Minos, in Crete.

# Chapter Three
# The Labyrinth

Everyone in Crete had heard of the brilliant craftsman Daedalus, and King Minos welcomed him warmly.

"I'm so happy you're here," he said. "I have a million and one jobs for you."

Daedalus set to work and, over the following years, he made many beautiful statues, pieces of furniture, vessels and even temples for

King Minos. He also made an astonishing labyrinth: a confusing maze of passages where the terrible man-eating Minotaur was kept.

For years all went well for Daedalus and Icarus. They were never short of work and became well-respected and prosperous. Then Theseus arrived from Athens and everything changed. By some miracle, Theseus man-aged to kill the Minotaur and, even worse, he escaped from the labyrinth. King Minos was

beside himself with fury and blamed his
escape on Daedalus.

"You promised me that it was impossible
to find your way out of the labyrinth. You're
an idiot and a traitor!" he cried.

In revenge, King Minos ordered his guards
to lock Daedalus into the labyrinth.

"Lock him into the labyrinth, and don't

forget to chuck his idiotic son in with him,"
he yelled. "And make sure you throw away
the key. Let them end their days in the dark,
with the rats!"

# Chapter Four
## Wings!

Foolish King Minos! How could he think that Daedalus, the designer of the labyrinth, would not know how to find his way out? Even in the dark and with the rats gnawing at his toes, Daedalus could escape.

But now that they were out of the labyrinth, what would they do? Daedalus knew that as soon as King Minos discovered their escape, he would have them hunted down and killed. They didn't have much time.

"There must be some way, Son," said Daedalus. "We are not defeated yet."

Then, looking up at the sky and the soaring seagulls, Daedalus came up with a clever plan.

"We'll fly away from Crete like birds, Icarus," he cried with relief.

"You're a genius, Dad!" his son replied.

So, using feathers bound with wax and twine, Daedalus made them each a pair of wonderful wings.

"A little wax here and a little twine there," he muttered to himself as he worked, "and a

feather or two. Yes, yes! These are going to be perfect!"

At last the wings were ready. As he strapped Icarus's wings onto his back, Daedalus warned his son, "Do not fly too close to the sea or your wings will get wet. Nor too close to the sun, or the wax will melt and you will fall."

"I'm going to be a bird and soar into the sky!" cried his son, flapping his arms up and down.

"Icarus, keep still and listen," his father said. "Wet wings won't work."

"I know, Father, and featherless wings won't fly!"

"Too true – and don't you forget it. Now, are you ready?" he asked his son. "It's time for take-off!"

## Chapter Five
# The Flight

Bravely, father and son threw themselves off the cliff-top and out over the Aegean Sea. At first their wings wobbled and they lost height,

but soon Daedalus and Icarus both began to rise into the air, soaring away from Crete.

"Stay close to me, Icarus," called Daedalus over the sound of the wind.

"Ooops, I've got wing-wobble, Dad!" laughed Icarus.

Sailors in ships below were amazed – they thought they must be seeing gods.

"There go Zeus and Hermes," they cried. "Lucky them! Flying looks such fun."

Icarus was certainly having fun. To begin with, he was slightly unsure of himself and stayed close behind his father, but soon he was overwhelmed with the joy of flying. He found it impossible to contain himself.

"Wheeee!" he went, as he flew past

Daedalus with a rush of feathers. "Zoóm!" he went as he swooped back and forth in front and then behind his father.

"Here I am, catch me if you can," he cried, forgetting everything his father had said to him.

"Come back, Icarus," his dad cried. "Remember my warnings!"

Higher and higher Icarus rose, further and further from his father and closer and closer to the sun…

"Hello, birds," he called. "Goodbye, birds."

"You know what pride comes before? Stop playing games, Icarus!" shouted his father. "Icarus, Icarus, where are you?" he called, but it was in vain for Icarus was lost in the miracle of flight.

# Chapter Six
## The Fall

Up and up went Icarus until there wasn't a single bird or cloud above him – only the sun. But still Icarus did not stop. He flew on until the sun's warmth embraced him. He hardly

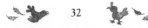

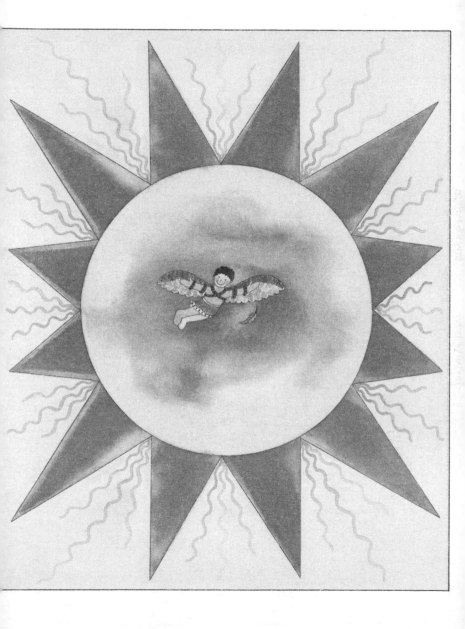

 33

noticed how hot he was getting, until he saw
the wax beginning to melt on his wings and
feathers floating all around him.

"Father, Father, help me!" he cried.

But his father was far below him and could
not hear his cries. All of a sudden, Icarus's
wings could no longer hold him and he
plunged towards the sea. Down and down he

went, below the birds, below the mountains, below the high temples, until he fell, like a dying comet, into the sea.

Meanwhile, Daedalus had lost sight of his son. He flew as high as he dared towards the sun, but he could see nothing. He flew back down towards the sea, where, to his dismay, he saw feathers floating on the waves.

"Oh, Icarus!" he cried. "My son! My only son."

Daedalus hovered over the sea until Icarus's body floated to the surface. Weeping all the while, Daedalus carried his dead son to a

nearby island. Finding a flower-strewn bank,
he gently laid Icarus's body down in a shallow
grave. As Daedalus smoothed the earth over
his son's resting place, a partridge landed by
his side. Daedalus realized that it was the spirit

of his nephew, Talos. He understood that the gods had punished him for killing Talos by allowing Icarus to fall to his death – just as Talos had done.

# Orpheus and Eurydice

# Chapter One
## The Death of Eurydice

Orpheus was young, handsome and brave,
but more importantly he was a wonderful
poet and musician. People came from all
over Greece to hear him play his lyre and sing.

His music made wild beasts tame, rivers

change their course, stones move closer
and trees bend to listen.

Orpheus loved the beautiful oak-

nymph, Eurydice, and luckily she loved him.
The day they married was the happiest in both
their lives. Orpheus believed that such happi-
ness must have come from the gods.

"They love my music, so they have blessed
us," he smiled happily.

Eurydice was as merry as the day was long.

As well as loving Orpheus, she loved dancing, singing and playing in the fields. Often, when Orpheus was busy, she would go out alone into the country.

One summer's day, as she danced merrily among the meadow flowers, she trod upon a deadly snake. The snake hissed in anger,

coiled up and sank its poisonous fangs into
her ankle. Eurydice didn't even have time to
cry out before she was overcome by the fatal
poison and fell to the ground … dead.

When Orpheus heard the news, he was
inconsolable. "I cannot live without you,
Eurydice!" he cried in torment.

# Chapter Two
## The Journey

For days and nights Orpheus would not eat, drink or sleep. His friends could do nothing to console him and began to fear for his life. Then, one dark and windy night, Orpheus took up his lyre and, without a word to anyone, left the house.

He travelled for months, over land and sea,

across rivers and mountains, so that his body ached and his lyre grew heavy on his shoulders. But at last he reached his destination, Hades, the land of the dead.

A land where the living never venture, for few – if any – return alive. Yet Orpheus had dared to go and beg for the return of his beloved Eurydice. Without her, his life held no meaning.

On the edge of the underworld flows the River Styx, where Charon, the ferryman, waits to carry the dead across its dark flowing depths.

"Charon, come, carry me across the river," Orpheus called to the tall, gaunt figure.

But Charon stayed on the far bank. "I only carry the dead," his voice echoed. "Go home, Orpheus, while you still can."

Charon continued to refuse to take Orpheus until he played him a tune on his lyre. Only then did Charon relent.

"You'll regret this," Charon warned, rowing the boat across the deep, black waters.

# Chapter Three
## Hades

When Charon dropped Orpheus on the other side of the river, Orpheus's journey quickly became a nightmare. The entrance to Hades was guarded by Cerberus, a three-headed dog, with serpents writhing out of its body and

eyes that glowed with fire. It lunged
towards Orpheus, saliva dripping from its
fangs – Orpheus was defenceless, without
sword or shield. He had only his lyre, which
he hastily began to play until gradually the
snarling, growling dog sank to the ground.
Three pairs of eyes began to droop and the
great beast rolled on its back in an ecstasy
of contentment!

Orpheus tiptoed over the beast, still playing his lyre, and passed through the gates of Hades.

Now he had to travel through the Asphodel Meadows, which were dark and desolate and haunted by ghosts. There was no light, no colour, just a vast and whispering greyness with the rushing of spirits as they endlessly circled the fields.

Then on through Tartarus, where the

evil were tortured. Their screams echoed around Orpheus and even the sweet notes of his lyre could not drown them out.

Finally, Orpheus reached the centre of Hades and King Pluto's castle. Orpheus bravely entered through the great black doors and knelt before King Pluto and his queen, Persephone. They were both amazed that a living person should risk his life to reach their kingdom.

"Why have you come, Orpheus?" asked
King Pluto.

"I have come to fetch my love, Eurydice,"
replied Orpheus. "She was taken from me by
the bite of a serpent and I cannot live without
her."

"It is impossible to take the dead from
Hades," replied the king. "Nobody leaves.
Besides, the dead know nothing of love."

Orpheus took up his lyre and began to sing.

He sang of his great love for Eurydice. He
sang of her laughter, her soft golden hair and
her dancing feet. He sang of the daily joy of

waking up beside her and holding her safe in
his arms through the night. He sang of his loss
and his unbearable sorrow. So heartfelt was his
singing that Persephone was moved to tears
and even Pluto felt his eyes pricked by tears.

Encouraged by Persephone, Pluto agreed to
release Eurydice on one condition: Orpheus

was not to look back until he reached the world of the living. He was to go from Hades playing his lyre and Eurydice would follow, but Orpheus must not turn until they reached the sunshine and the land of the living.

"If you do," King Pluto emphasized, "you will never see Eurydice again."

## Chapter Four
# The Return Journey

So Orpheus departed without knowing whether Eurydice followed or not. He kept looking forwards and never for one moment did he stop playing his lyre. He travelled back through Tartarus, witnessing again the agony

of the tortured, but still he played and looked
ahead. He travelled through the Asphodel
Meadows, without turning or missing a note,
even though the ghosts whispered words of
doubt in his ears.

"Is she there?" they whispered. "How can
you be sure?"

"Look, look!" they urged. "Before it's too
late."

Orpheus ignored them and walked on,

playing his lyre. He passed Cerberus, who fell at his feet as the music calmed his three heads and even the hissing serpents were stilled.

Only as Orpheus neared the River Styx did doubts begin to enter his mind.

"Maybe, I'm a fool," he muttered to himself. "Maybe Eurydice isn't there at all."

Orpheus hesitated. What if Pluto and Persephone had tricked him? This was his

last chance to go back – once he had crossed the river he would never be able to return.

He could see Charon waiting for him with his boat, but was he waiting for Eurydice too?

Orpheus was so nearly out of Hades, he imagined that he could almost feel the sun on his face, surely it was safe to turn – better to be sure now, while he could still go back. With one foot in the boat, Orpheus turned.

There was his beloved Eurydice, not five paces behind. She was pale, but smiling upon him. Then, as Orpheus gasped with horror, her living form faded and Eurydice became a ghost of the underworld. As Charon slowly ferried Orpheus into the sunlit world, he felt his heart had been torn from his body as he realized that he had lost his love for ever.

# Other fabulous retellings by
# *Marcia Williams*

# Available from all good booksellers

www.walker.co.uk